Sea Life Adult Coloring Book

Realistic Adult Coloring Book, Advanced Sea Life Coloring Book for Adults: Fish, Ocean, Nature, Marine Life.

Realistic Animal Coloring Book: Vol 5

by Amanda Davenport

ISBN-13: 978-1530568895

ISBN-10: 1530568897

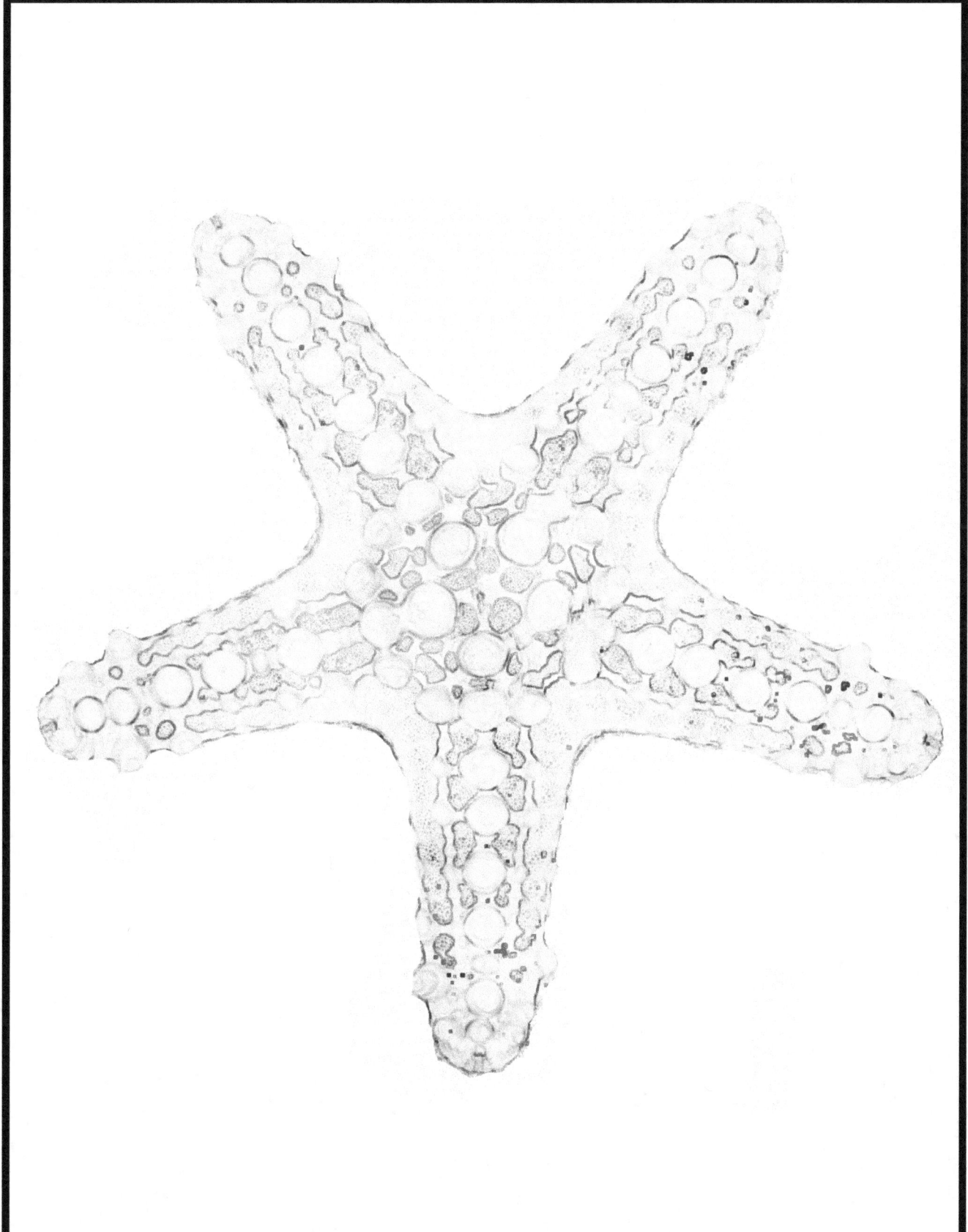

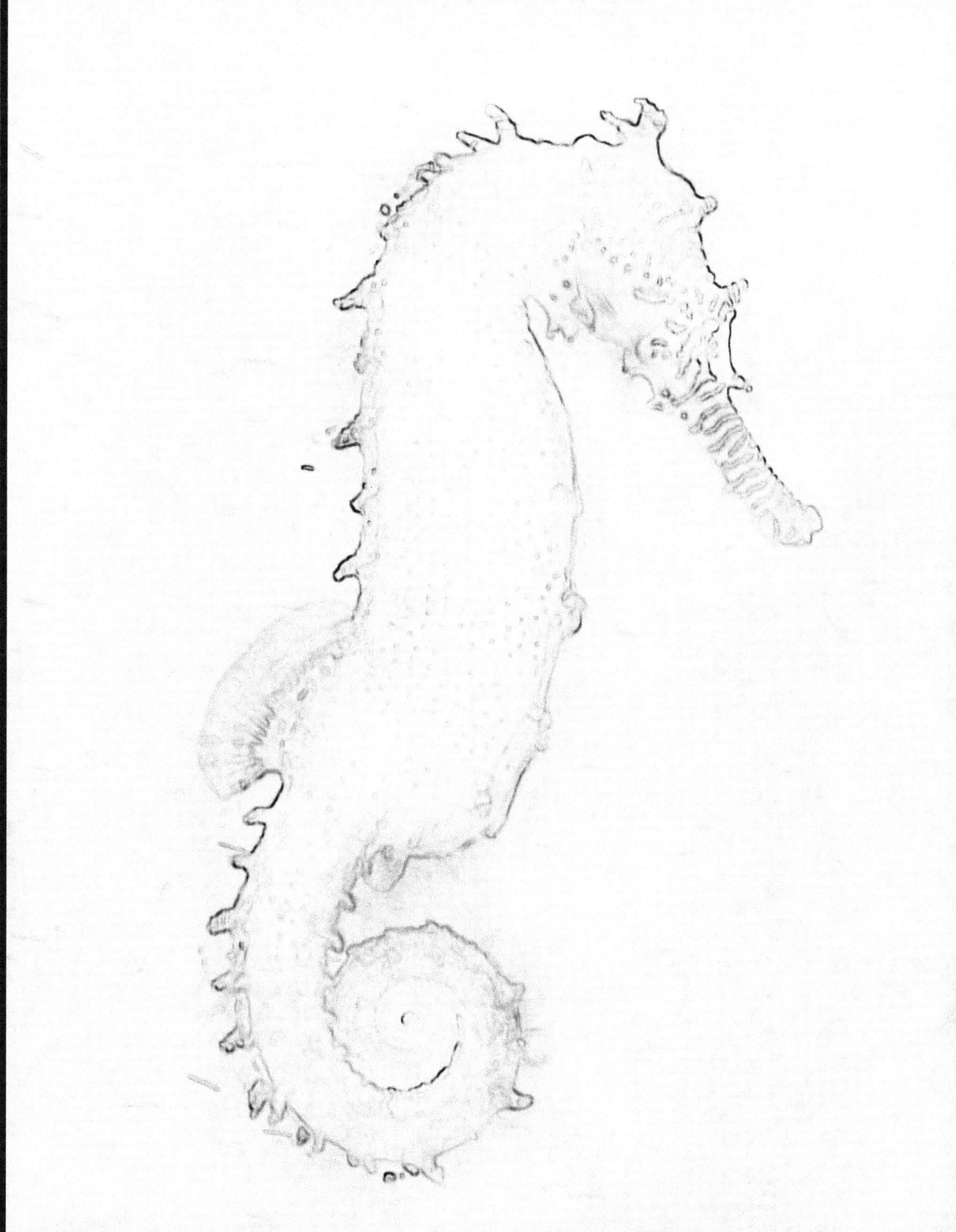

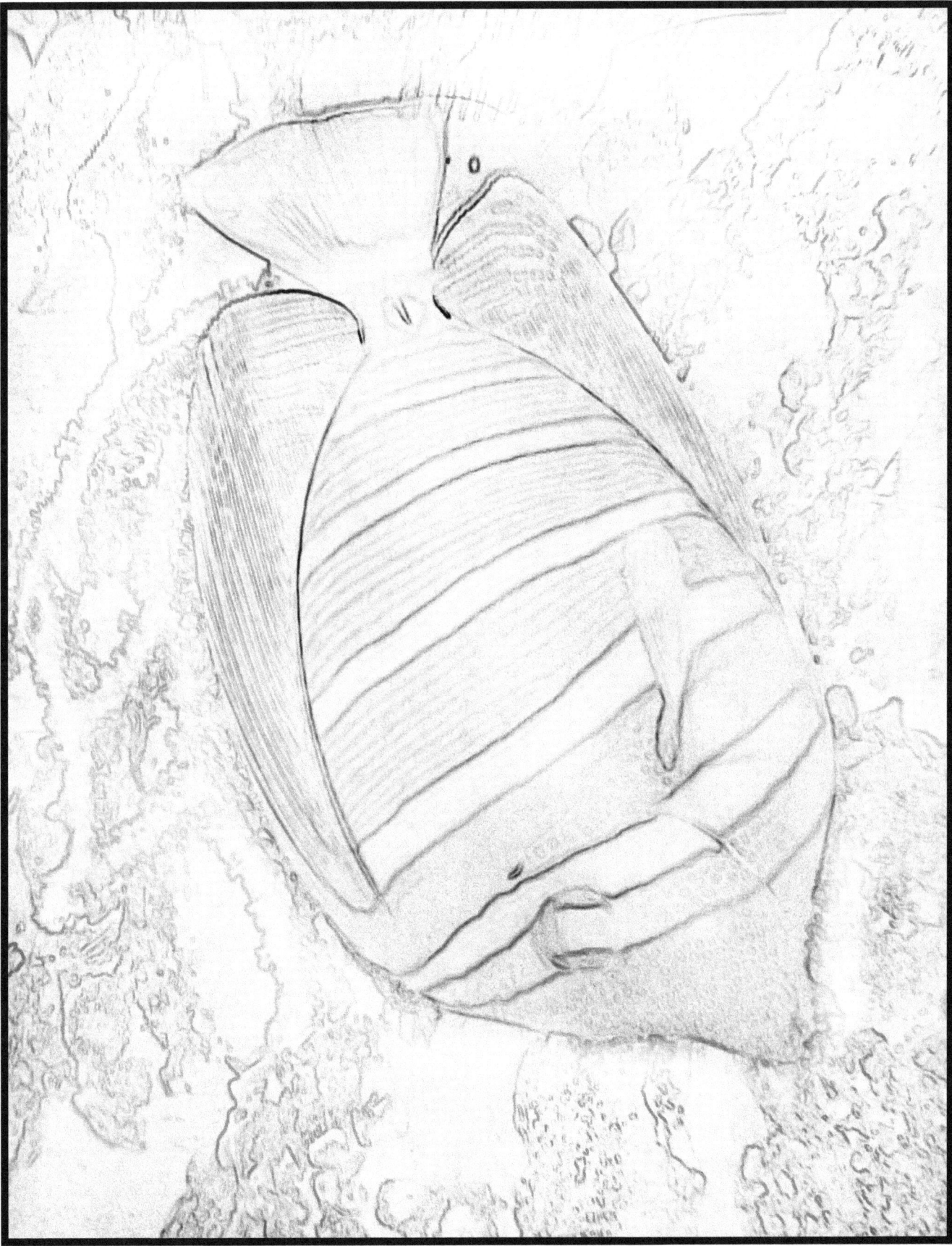

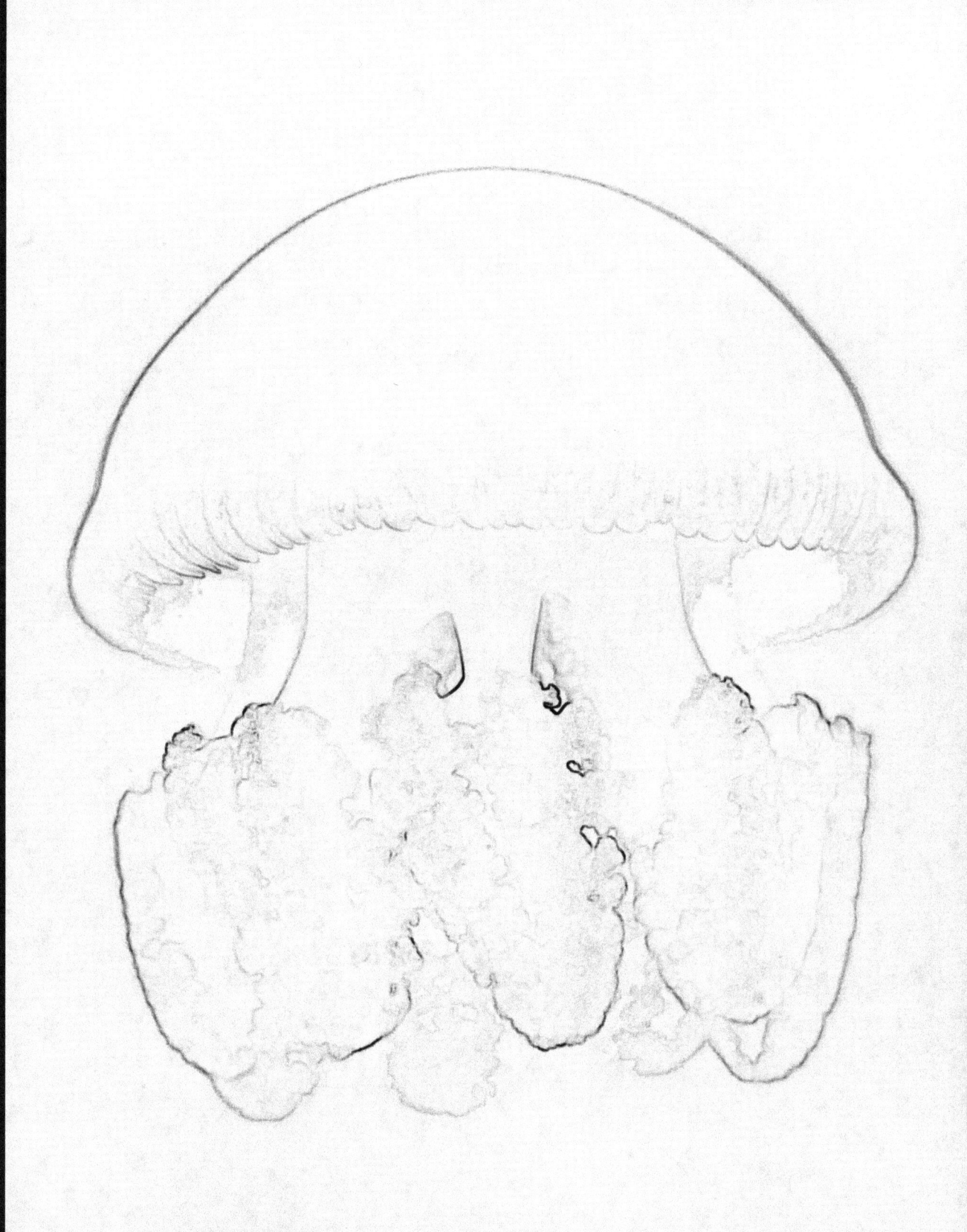

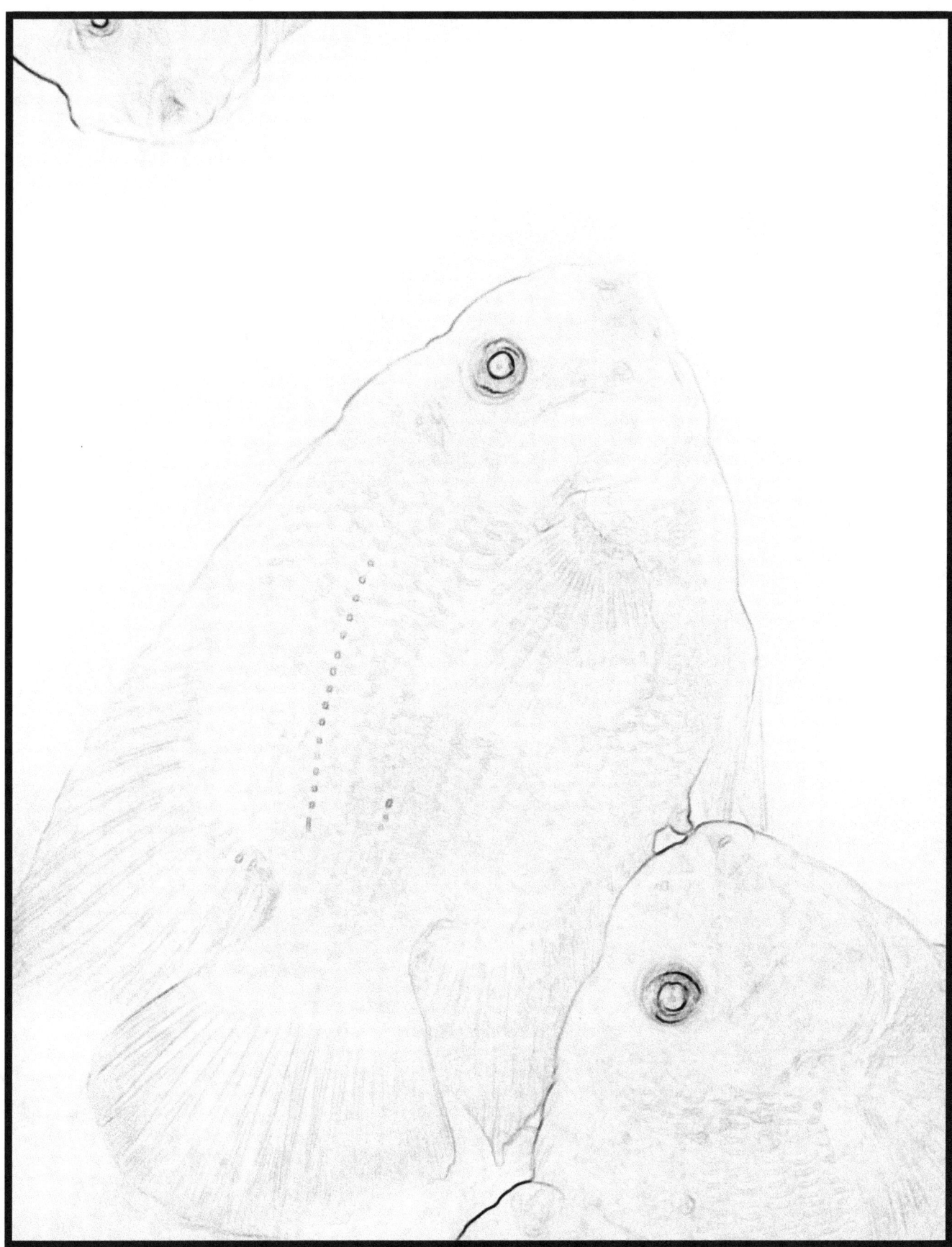

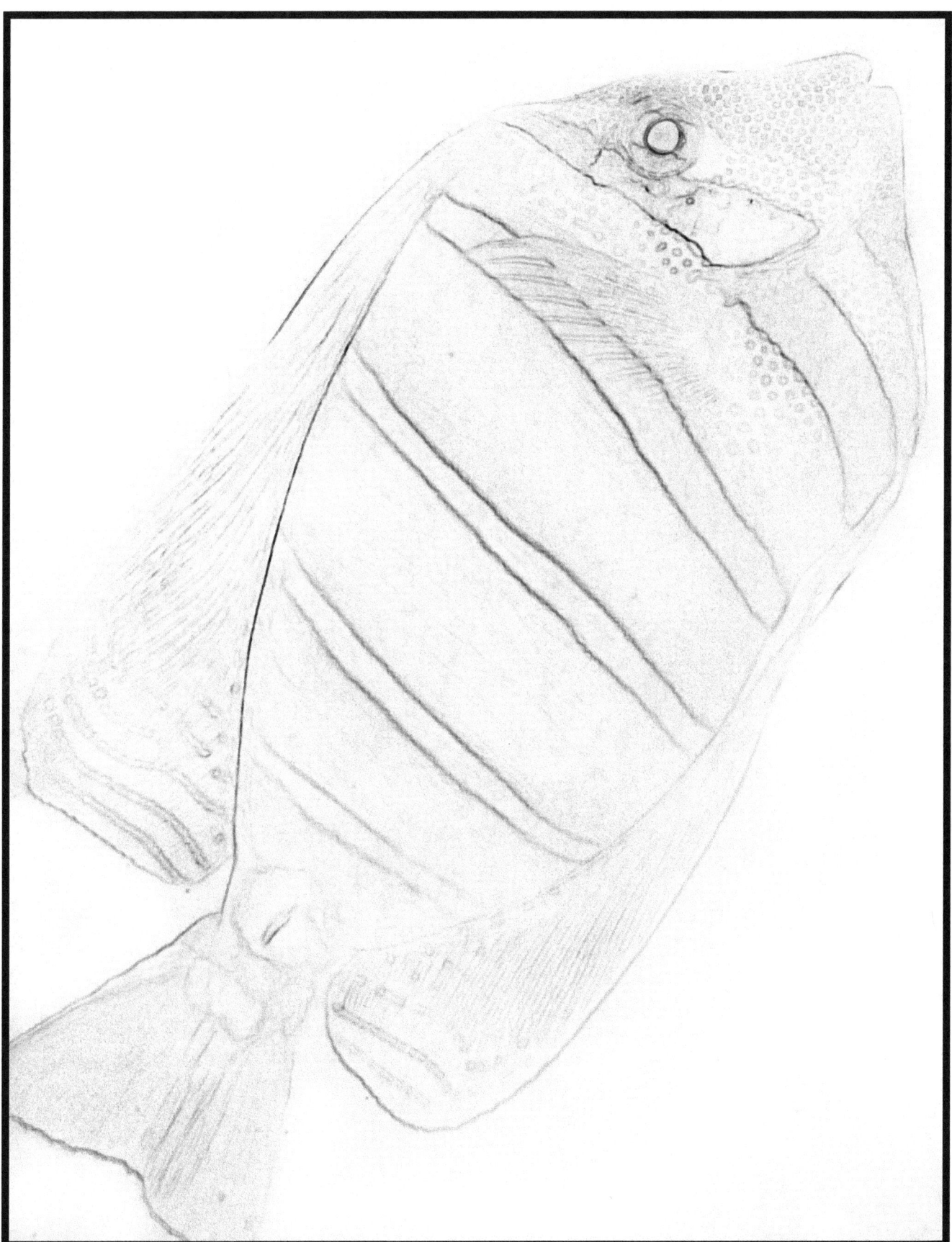

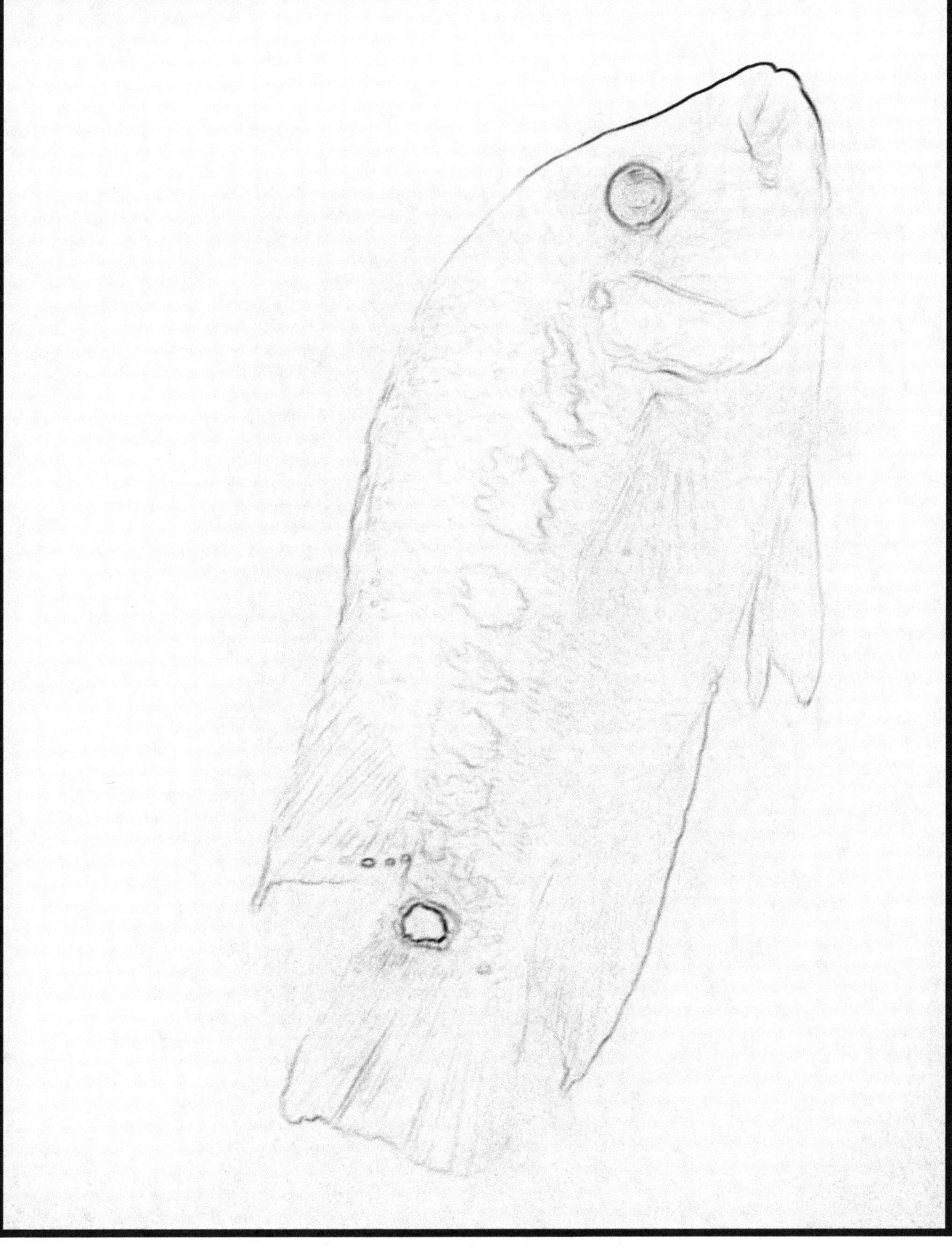

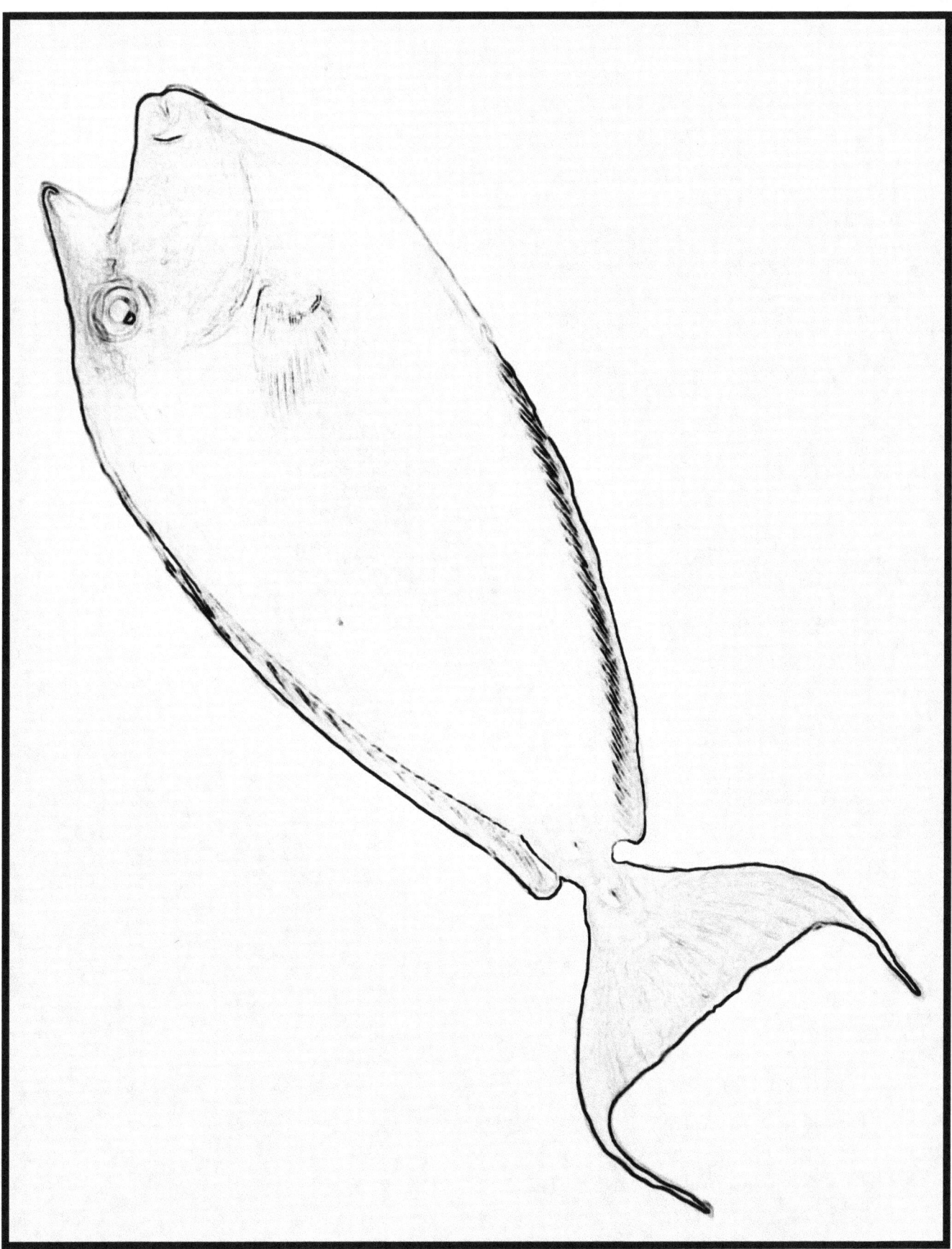

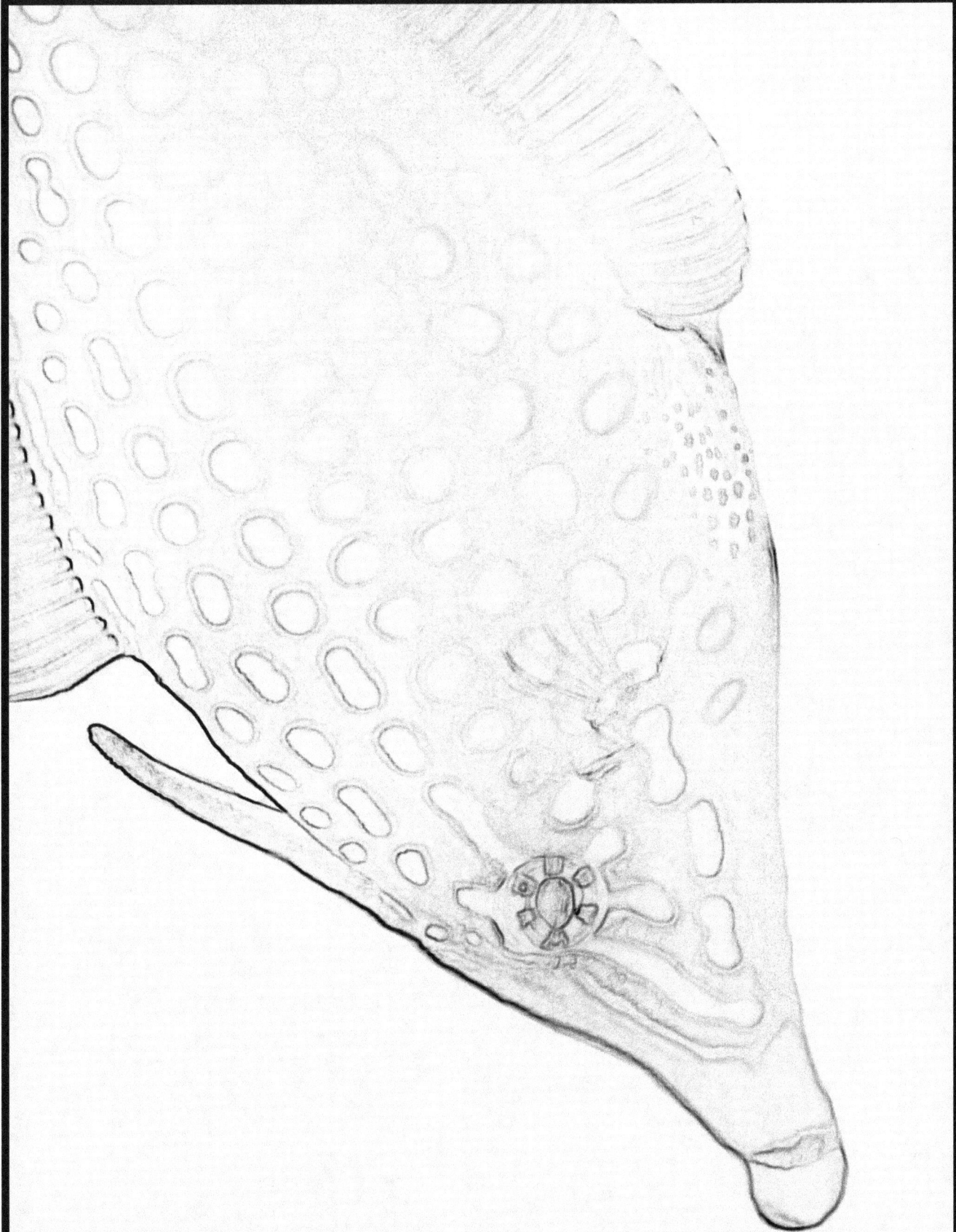

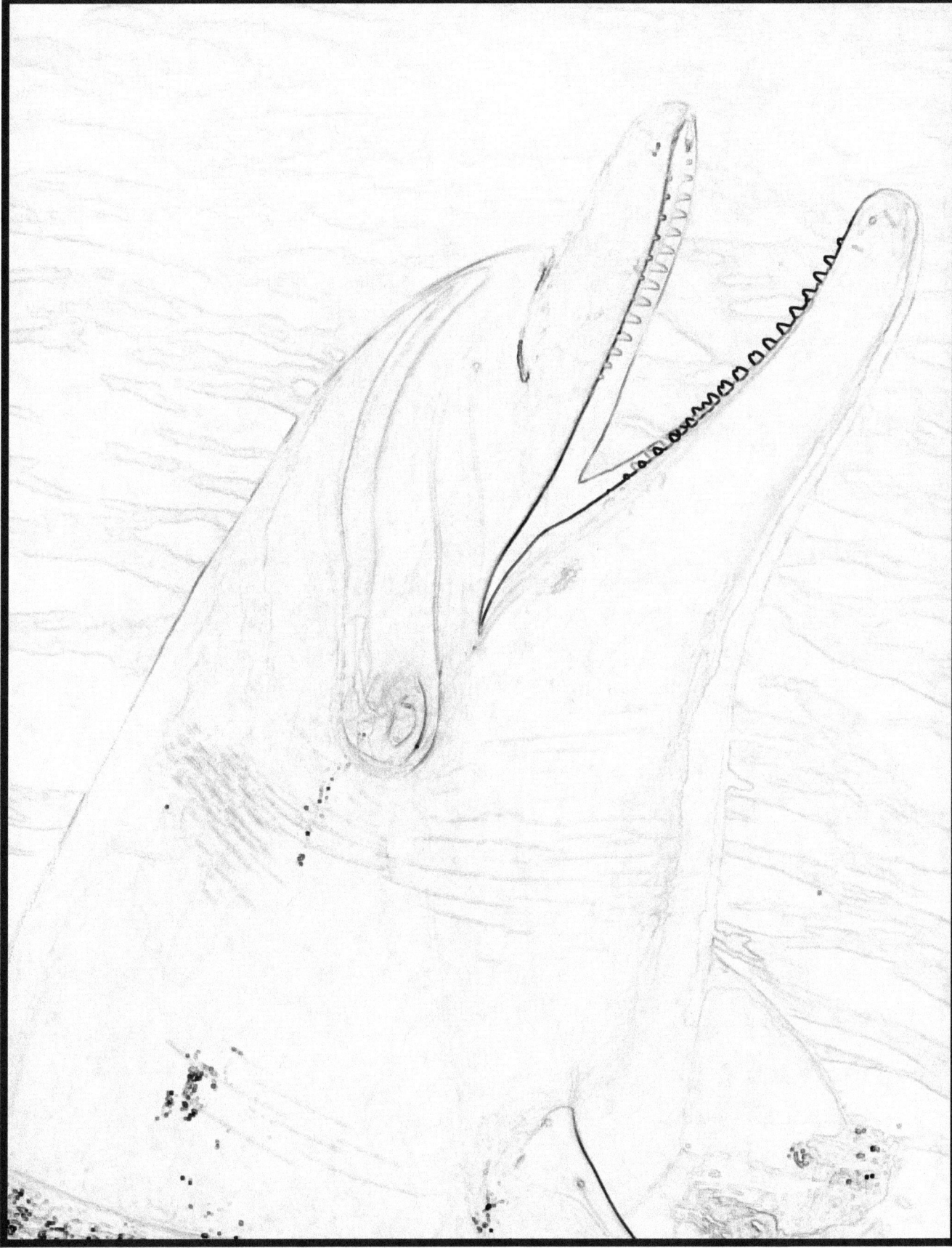

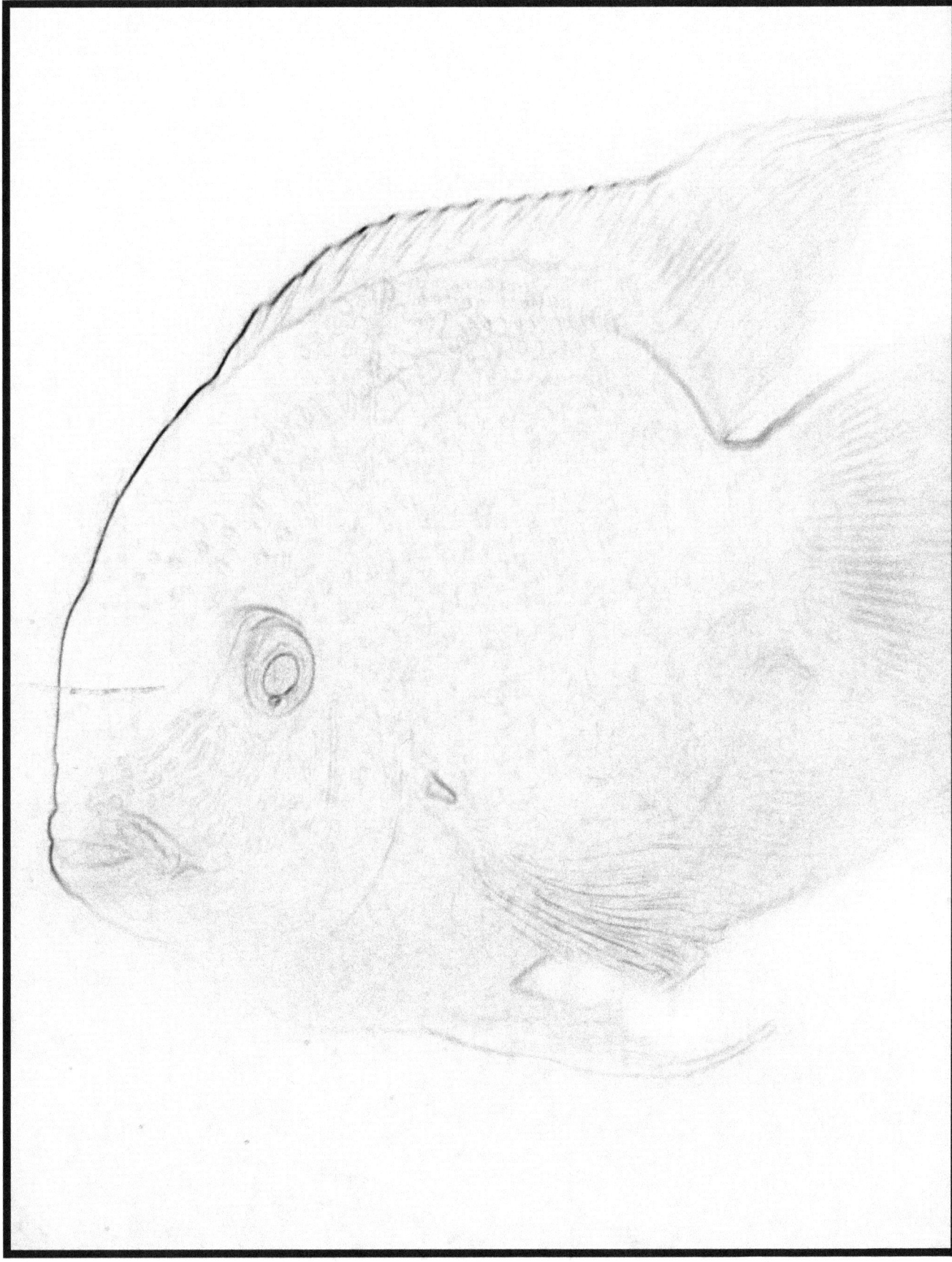

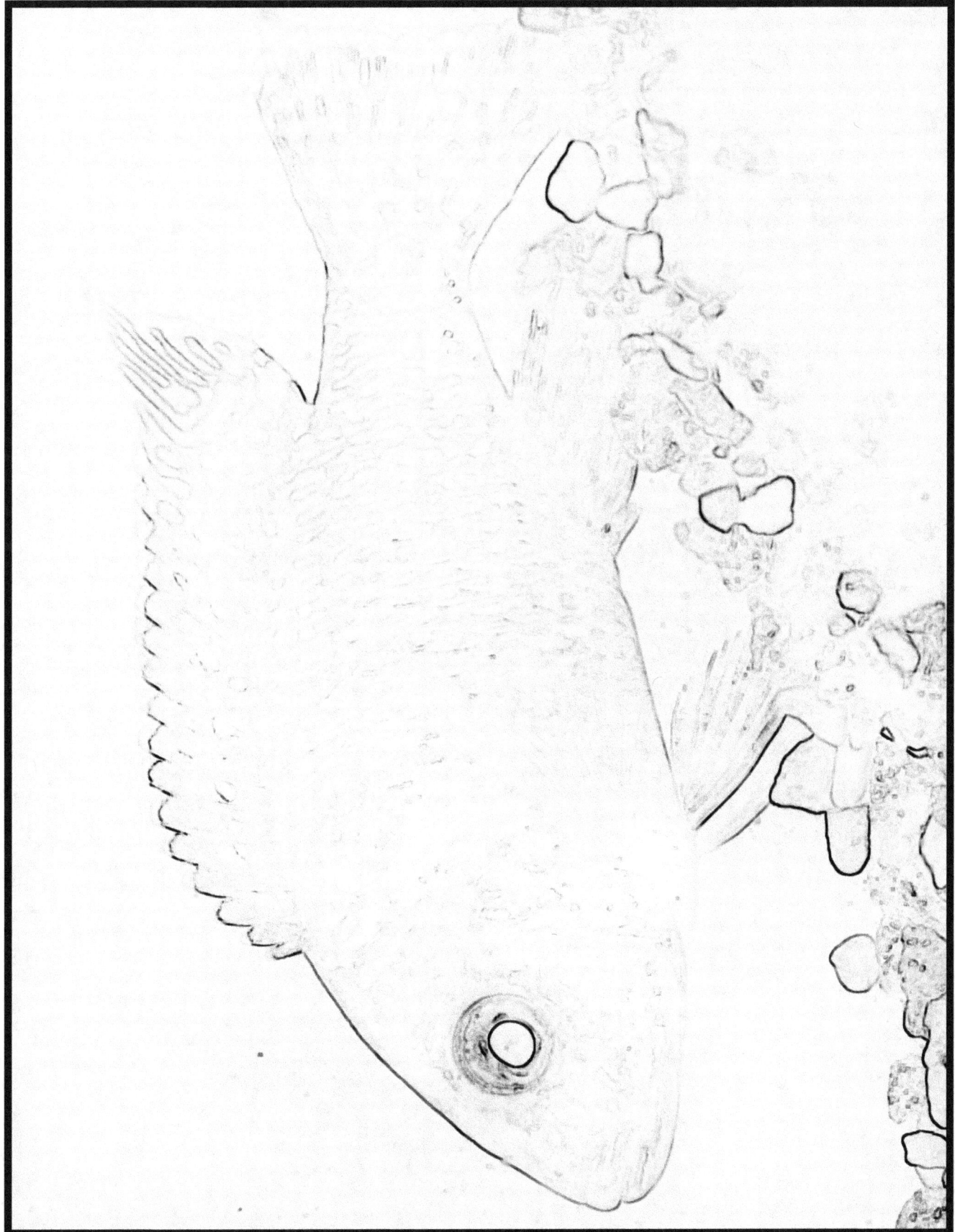

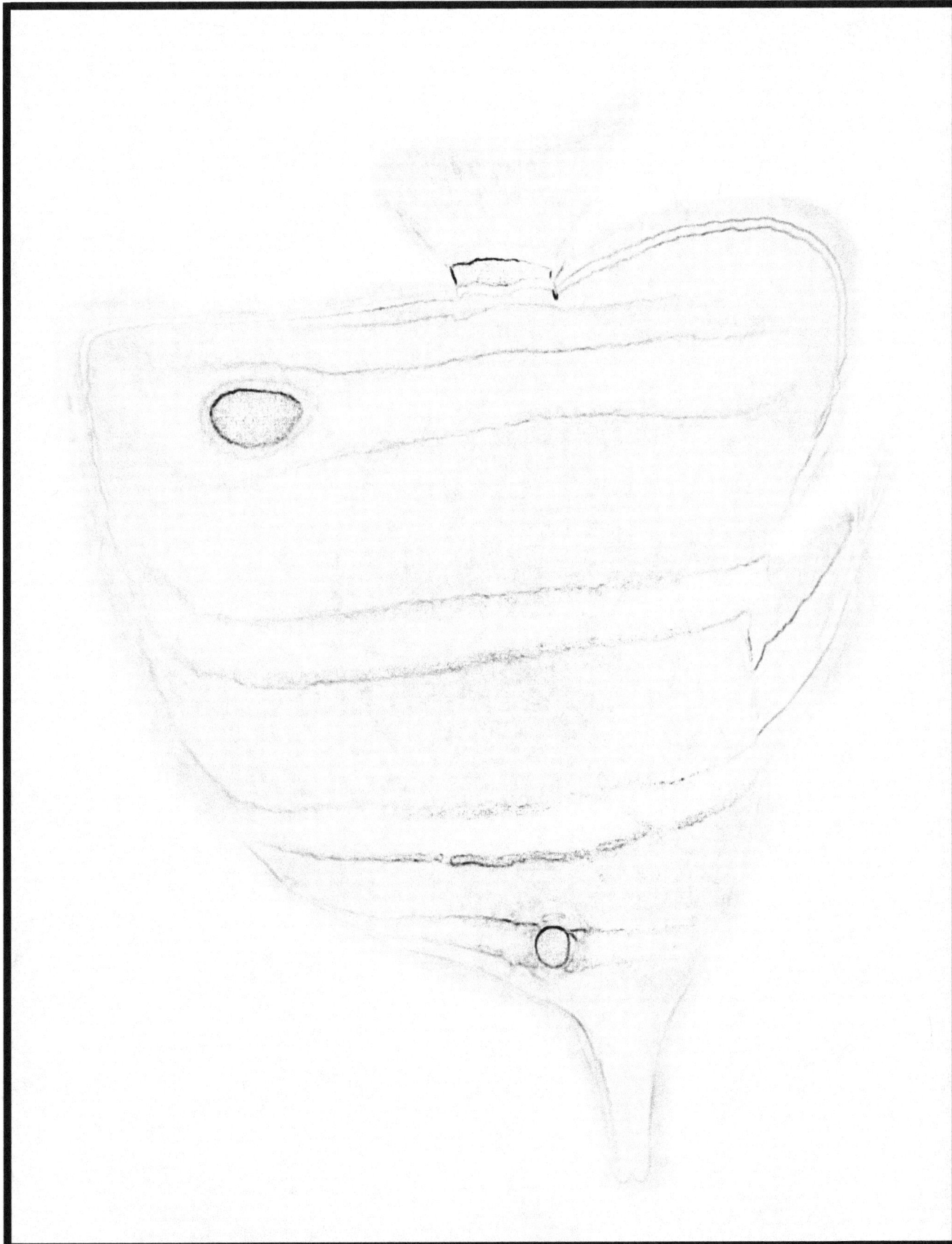

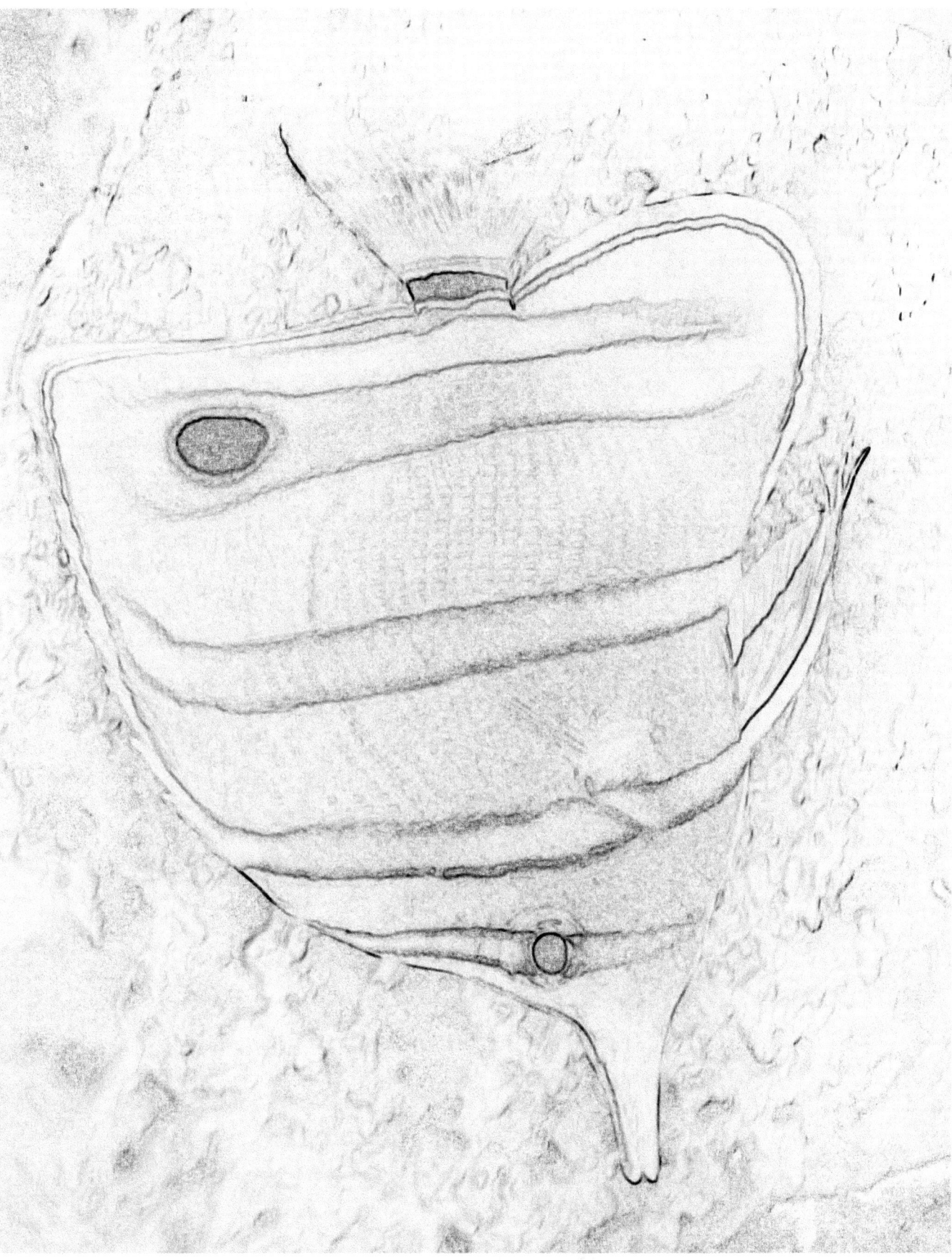

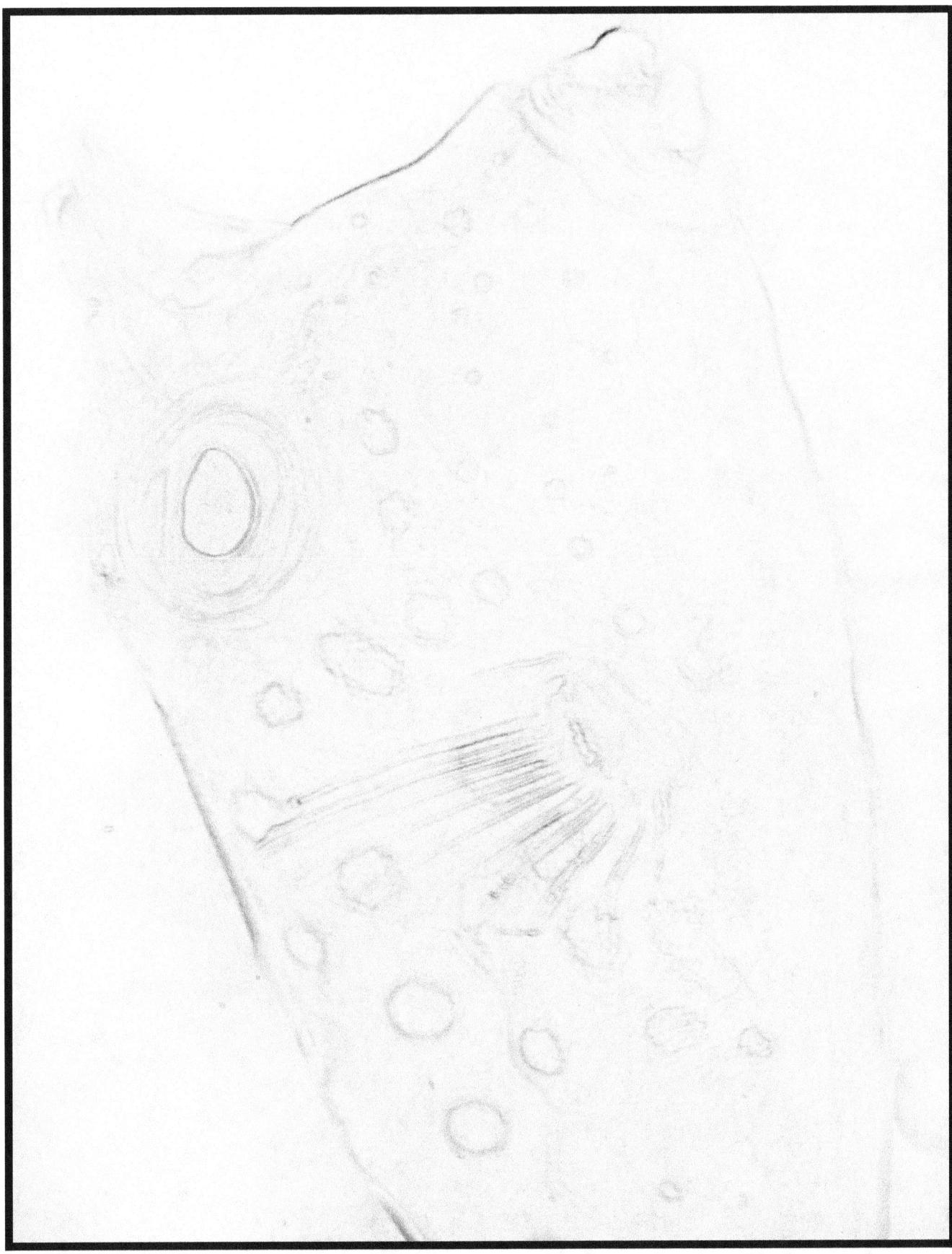

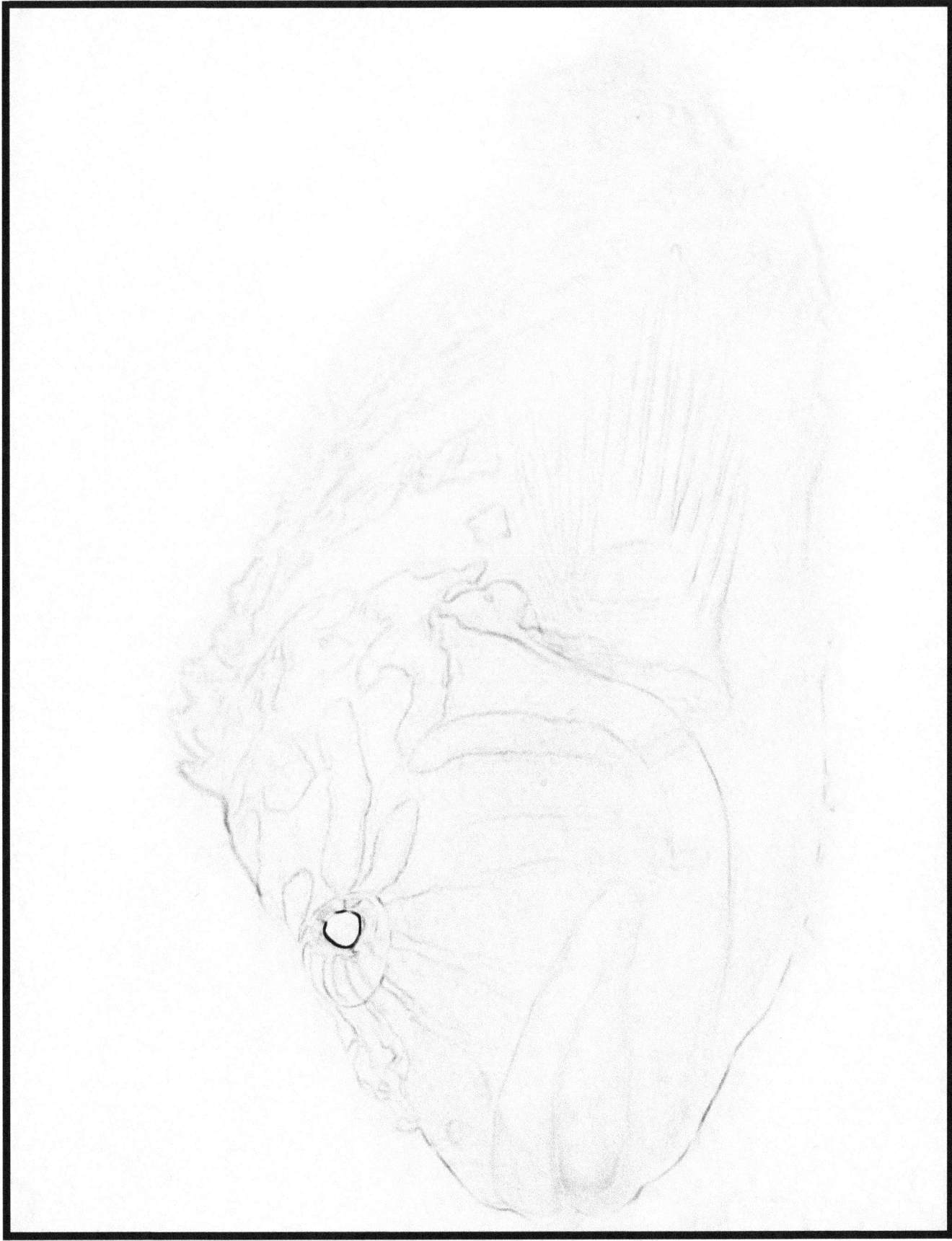

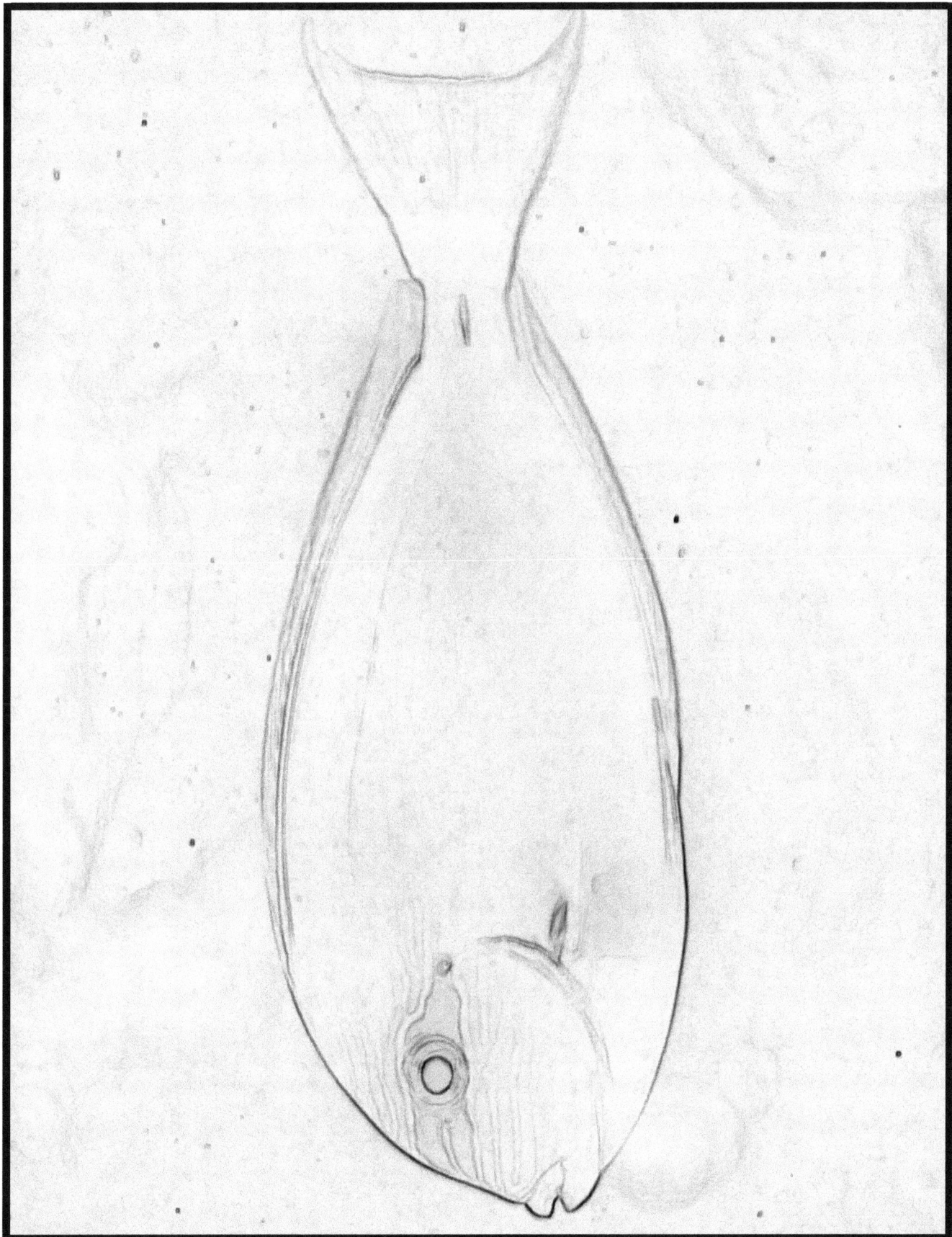

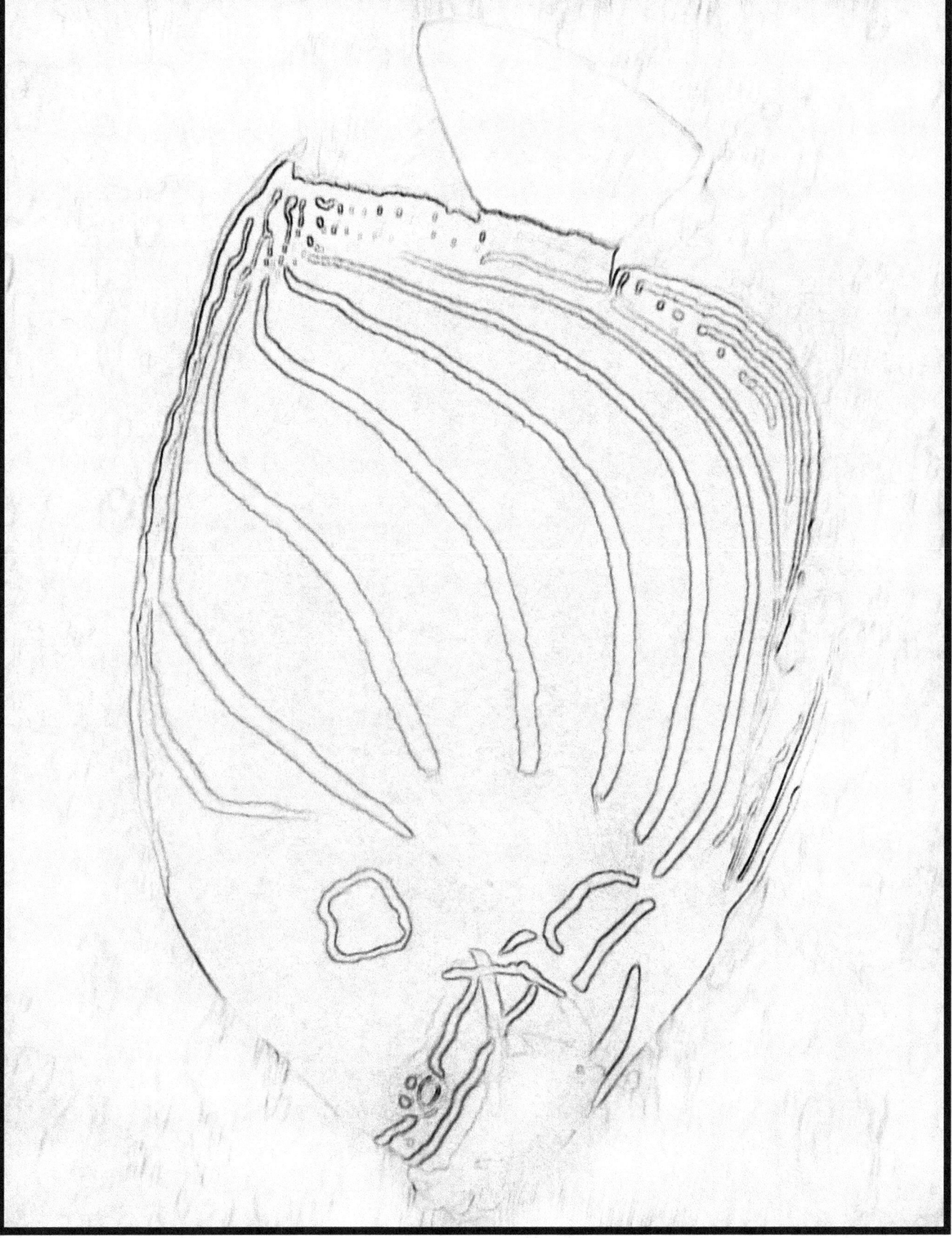

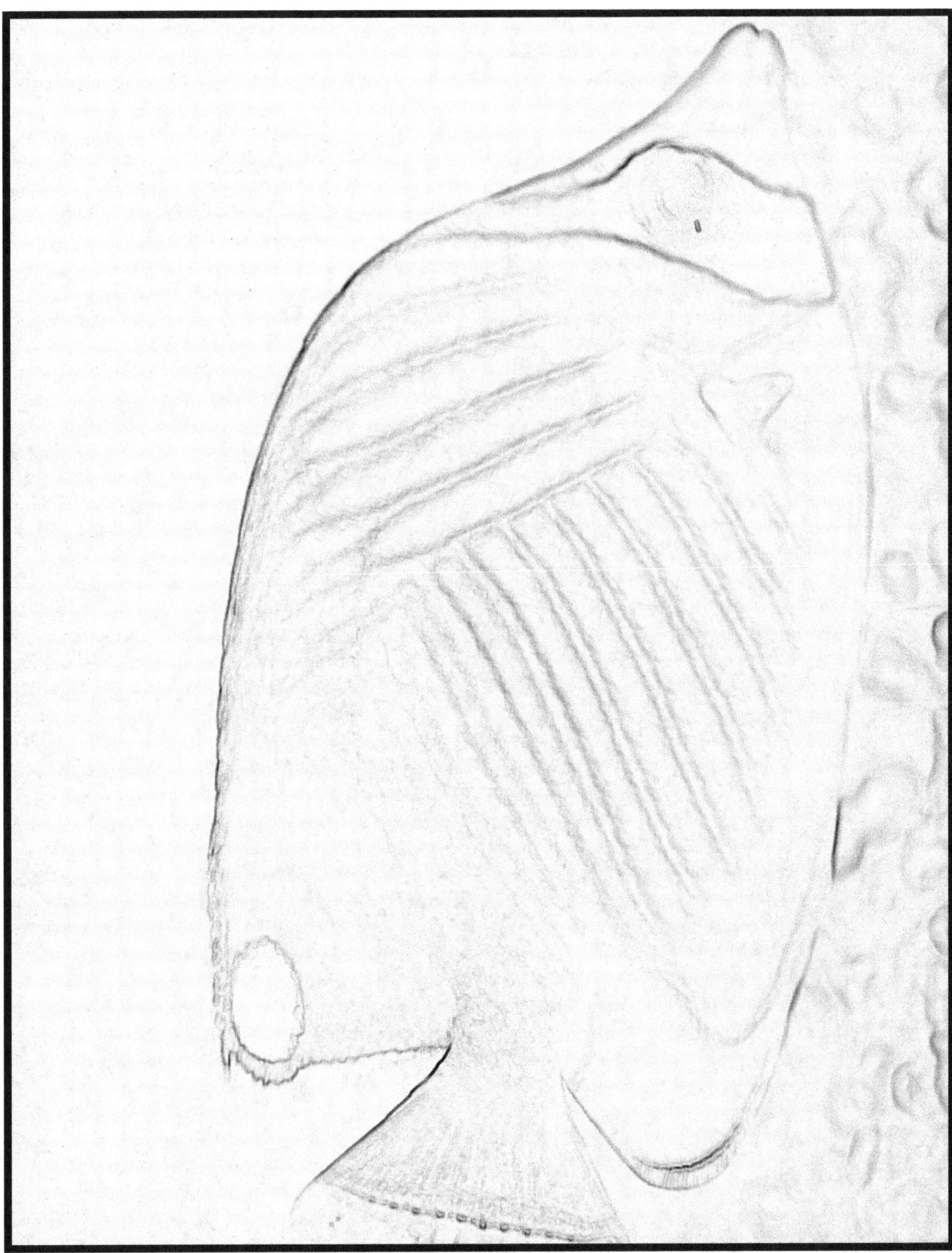

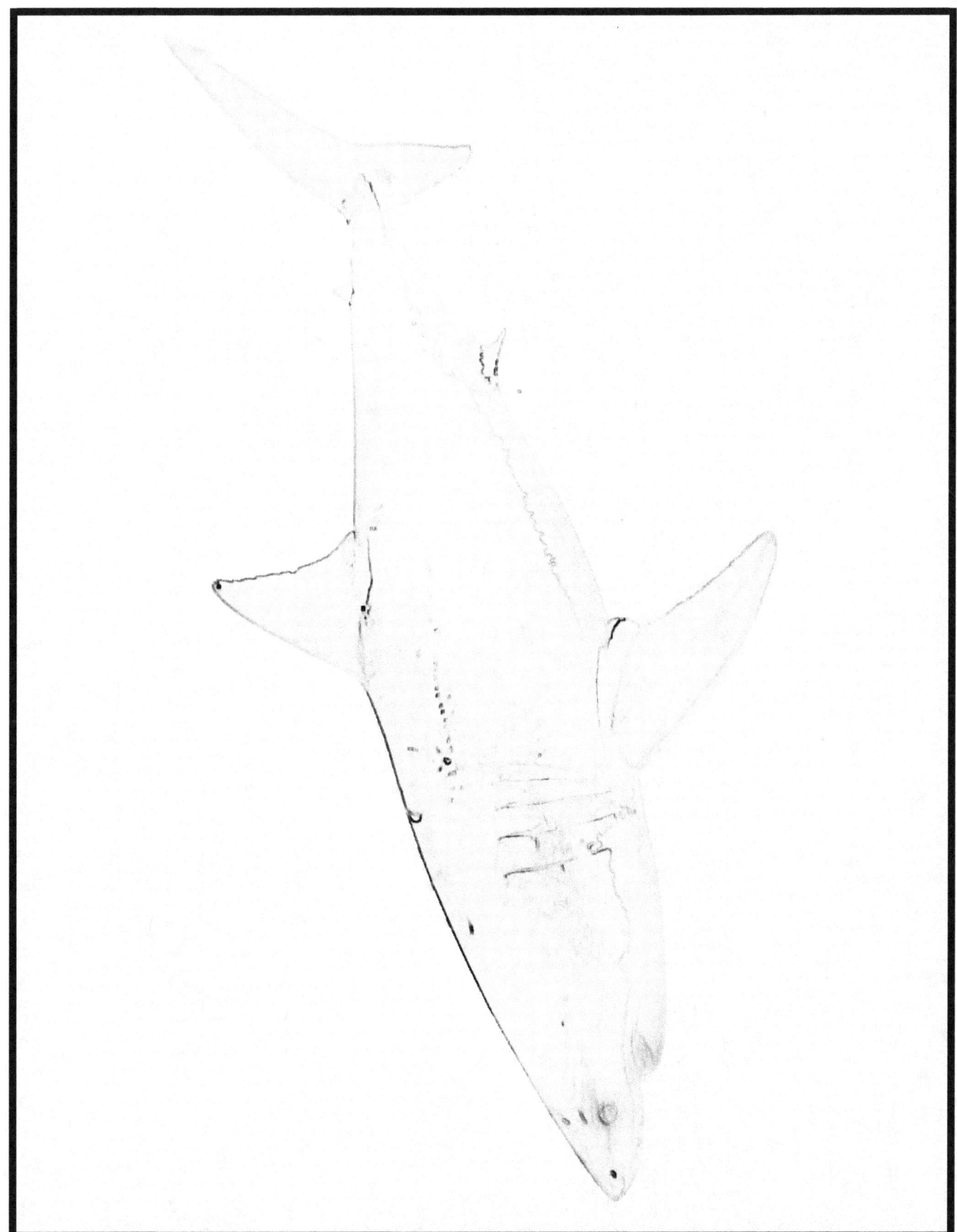

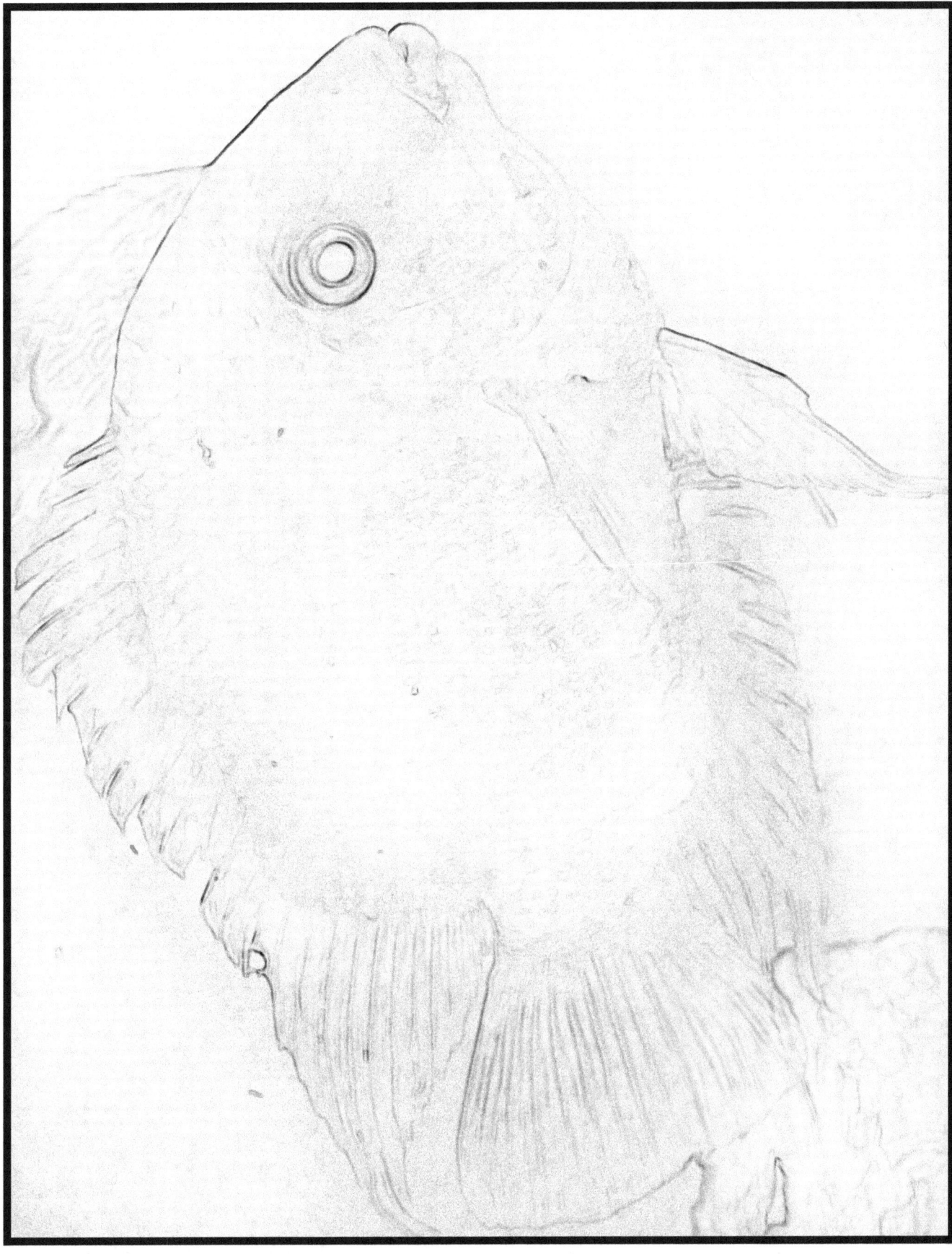

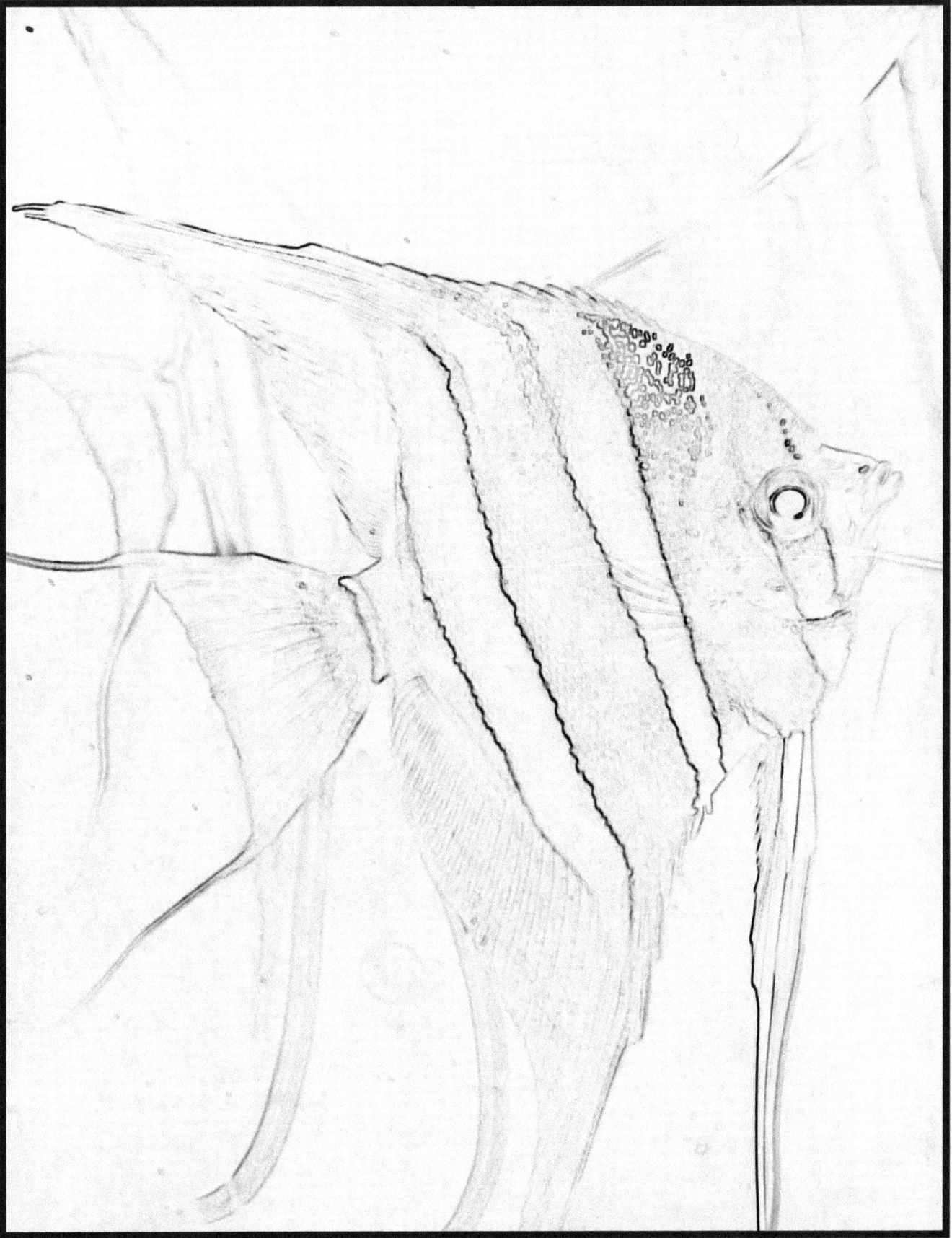

www.ingramcontent.com/pod-product-compliance
Lightning Source LLC
Chambersburg PA
CBHW081419280526

45788CB00009B/3154